SUMMARY

of

Jocko Willink & **Leif Babin's**

EXTREME OWNERSHIP

How U.S. Navy SEALs
Lead and Win

BY
CHRIS LAMBERTSEN

Summary of *Extreme Ownership: How US Navy SEALs Lead and Win*
by Jocko Willink and Leif Babin

Copyright © 2020 by Chris Lambertsen

All Rights Reserved. No part of this book may be reproduced in any manner without the express written consent of the author, except in the case of brief excerpts in critical reviews or articles.

Paperback ISBN: 978-0-9898229-6-1
Also available as an e-book

Disclaimer: All Rights Reserved. No part of this publication may be reproduced or retransmitted, electronic or mechanical, without the written permission of the publisher; with the exception of brief quotes used in connection in reviews written for inclusion in a magazine or newspaper. This eBook is licensed for your personal enjoyment only. This eBook may not be re-sold or given away to other people. If you would like to share this book with another person, please purchase an additional copy for each recipient. If you're reading this book and did not purchase it, or it was not purchased for your use only, then please purchase your own copy.

Product names, logos, brands, and other trademarks featured or referred to within this publication are the property of their respective trademark holders. These trademark holders are not affiliated with us and they do not sponsor or endorse our publications. This book is unofficial and unauthorized. It is not authorized, approved, licensed, or endorsed by the aforementioned interests or any of their licensees. The information in this book has been provided for educational and entertainment purposes only. The information contained in this book has been compiled from sources deemed reliable and it is accurate to the best of the Author's knowledge; however, the Author cannot guarantee its accuracy and validity and cannot be held liable for any errors or omissions. Upon using the information contained in this book, you agree to hold harmless the author from and against any damages, costs, and expenses, including any legal fees, potentially resulting from the application of any of the information provided by this guide.

The disclaimer applies to any damages or injury caused by the use and application, whether directly or indirectly, of any advice or information presented, whether for breach of contract, tort, neglect, personal injury, criminal intent, or under any other cause of action. You agree to accept all risks of using the information presented inside this book. The fact that an individual or organization is referred to in this document as a citation or source of information does not imply that the author or publisher endorses the information that the individual or organization provided. This is an unofficial summary & analytical review and has not been approved by the original author of the book.

NOTE TO READERS

This is an unofficial summary & analysis of *Extreme Ownership: How U.S. Navy SEALs Lead and Win* by Jocko Willink and Leif Babin. This summary is designed to enrich your reading experience.

CONTENTS

Introduction vii

PART I: WINNING THE WAR WITHIN

CHAPTER 1: Extreme Ownership 3
CHAPTER 2: No Bad Teams, Only Bad Leaders 9
CHAPTER 3: Believe 15
CHAPTER 4: Check the Ego 21

PART II: THE LAWS OF COMBAT

CHAPTER 5: Cover and Move 29
CHAPTER 6: Simple 33
CHAPTER 7: Prioritize and Execute 39
CHAPTER 8: Decentralized Command 45

PART III: SUSTAINING VICTORY

CHAPTER 9: Plan 53
CHAPTER 10: Leading Up and Down the Chain
of Command 59
CHAPTER 11: Decisiveness Amid Uncertainty 65
CHAPTER 12: Discipline Equals Freedom—
The Dichotomy of Leadership 71

> *"Discipline equals freedom."*
>
> **—JOCKO WILLINK,** *Extreme Ownership:
> How U.S. Navy SEALs Lead and Win*

INTRODUCTION

THIS BOOK IS WRITTEN by Leif Babin and Jocko Willink, two former US Navy SEALs who served combat tours in Iraq and now run a successful consulting firm that helps organizations develop leaders. Each chapter begins by relating a story from their time in combat and/or as SEAL trainers which illustrates particular leadership challenges, concepts, and solutions, followed by a list of "Principles" that are enumerated in this summary as "Lessons." Finally, the authors tie the concepts in the chapter to a practical business scenario that they have come across in their career as consultants, showing how these principles also apply to leadership in the civilian world.

While there are three sections to this book and 12 chapters that cover a range of concepts, the overall lesson is that leaders must practice "Extreme Ownership:" the idea that a leader is ultimately responsible and accountable for everything within his or her sphere of influence. Good leaders assess goals and problems, hold themselves accountable for what they can control—and find ways to positively shape the situation.

> "The test is not a complex one: when the alarm goes off, do you get up out of bed, or do you lie there in comfort and fall back to sleep? If you have the discipline to get out of bed, you win—you pass the test. If you are mentally weak for that moment and you let that weakness keep you in bed, you fail. Though it seems small, that weakness translates to more significant decisions. But if you exercise discipline, that too translates to more substantial elements of your life."
>
> —**JOCKO WILLINK,** *Extreme Ownership: How U.S. Navy SEALs Lead and Win*

PART I

WINNING THE WAR WITHIN

> "Implementing Extreme Ownership requires checking your ego and operating with a high degree of humility. Admitting mistakes, taking ownership, and developing a plan to overcome challenges are integral to any successful team."
>
> **—JOCKO WILLINK,** *Extreme Ownership: How U.S. Navy SEALs Lead and Win*

CHAPTER 1

EXTREME OWNERSHIP

By Jocko Willink

JOCKO RECOUNTS A SCENARIO he faced in Iraq that stemmed from "confusion, inaccurate information, broken communications, and mayhem."

His unit of SEALs along with Iraqi and other US forces was charged with clearing a neighborhood of insurgents, building by building. A conventional team encountered stiff resistance and called for a quick reaction force (QRF; back-up). Shortly after, a team of SEALs was in deeper trouble and called for a "heavy quick reaction force," which included tanks. As the SEAL commander, Jocko went with the heavy QRF.

The tank was about to fire into a building but in Jocko's opinion "something didn't add up." He personally checked out the building and found the SEAL sniper team that had called for help, not insurgents. It had been a "friendly fire incident;" the Iraqi soldiers had moved outside of their assigned area and attacked the house the SEALs were in. One Iraqi soldier had been killed and one SEAL wounded in the exchange. Everyone was shaken but pressed on, doing two more missions.

Despite the chaotic environment, Jocko felt responsible. Higher command shut down all SEAL operations until the incident was investigated, and the author thought his reputation was irreparably damaged, assuming they were looking for someone to blame.

He compiled a report of what had happened and why, including various units changing their plans without notification. But there were so many elements to what had gone wrong, he couldn't figure out where to assign blame.

Finally, he realized that the one person to blame was himself—the leader. Despite not having the ability to control all of the things other individuals had done wrong, he was responsible for them. He had to take complete ownership over everything that happened: "This is what a leader does—even if it means getting fired."

The author took responsibility and committed that he would do all that was possible for a friendly fire incident to never happen again. In retrospect, he believes that his willingness to be held accountable was the reason he *wasn't* fired.

LESSONS

- A leader is responsible for everything—good and bad—that happens with his team or organization. He or she needs to own mistakes and move forward by accounting for them while continuing the mission. **Jocko's term for this is "Extreme Ownership" and credits this culture for the success of SEAL leaders.** The principle is also applicable to good leaders in any endeavor, from business to sports.

- Leaders must never *blame* subordinates, instead they must first determine how leadership—the planning and coordination of the mission—may have led to failure. Underperforming subordinates must be trained and mentored—and if they don't improve, it is the leader's responsibility to remove them. The mission and the team are the priorities.

- People often blame failures on bad luck or make other excuses. Assuming responsibility takes "extraordinary humility and courage," and a good leader will put focus toward improving the performance of the team.

- When analyzing failures, leaders must be objective. There is no room for ego, emotion, or personal angles. This analysis should be dedicated to facts that enable the leader and the team to perform better in the future.

- Leaders should never take credit for success; instead, giving this credit to subordinates. This creates a culture that subordinates emulate, thus taking extreme ownership of the pieces of the puzzle that they are responsible for.

IN BUSINESS

Jocko cites an example in which he provided executive coaching to a company's vice president who had failed to meet manufacturing goals set by the board. The VP had to implement a new plan to consolidate plants, make the manufacturing process more efficient, and create an incentives program that increased productivity. After about a year, not much of the plan had been executed and the VP's job was on the line.

While the VP was smart, he made excuses for his failure to execute the plan, listing various factors. Chief among them was resistance from subordinate leaders in sales and manufacturing. Jocko explained the concept of extreme ownership to the executive and helped rehearse a briefing to the board in which he took complete responsibility and outlined specific steps to get the plan moving.

The vice president was the leader—and if he couldn't influence people to do what he needed them to do, he was not displaying effective leadership. The VP offered initial resistance to taking extreme ownership, but eventually subsumed his ego and made plans to adapt, briefing the board on a "no-nonsense list of corrective measures."

ADDITIONAL PRINCIPLES

- When a leader blames others the attitude spreads, planning isn't improved, and the team fails.

- If a subordinate doesn't execute and the leader isn't *directly* responsible, the leader still must assume that he or she communicated poorly or the subordinate requires more training, for example. In any case, the leader remains responsible.

- Subordinates respect extreme ownership.

- Good leaders own failures and find ways to improve. This results in teams that dominate teams led by leaders who make excuses.

"Leaders should never be satisfied. They must always strive to improve, and they must build that mind-set into the team. They must face the facts through a realistic, brutally honest assessment of themselves and their team's performance. Identifying weaknesses, good leaders seek to strengthen them and come up with a plan to overcome challenges. The best teams anywhere, like the SEAL Teams, are constantly looking to improve, add capability, and push the standards higher. It starts with the individual and spreads to each of the team members until this becomes the culture, the new standard. The recognition that there are no bad teams, only bad leaders facilitates Extreme Ownership and enables leaders to build high-performance teams that dominate on any battlefield, literal or figurative."

—**JOCKO WILLINK,** *Extreme Ownership: How U.S. Navy SEALs Lead and Win*

CHAPTER 2

NO BAD TEAMS, ONLY BAD LEADERS

By Leif Babin

LEIF RECOUNTS HELL WEEK during a class of SEAL training: "seventy-two hours straight of nearly non-stop physical exertion." He was assisting Basic Underwater Demolition/SEAL Training (BUD/S) instructors during Hell Week, while also serving as an instructor for the Junior Officer Training Course.

BUD/S is incredibly difficult. In Leif's own previous training class of 101, only 40 had graduated. Several dozen men had quit or left the class he was overseeing after becoming sick or injured. The training is not just a physical test, rather a mental one that assesses strength of will, communication, teamwork, and leadership.

Trainees are grouped into boat crews of seven men who carry a heavy "inflatable boat, small (IBS)," often filled with water and sand. They must run with it for miles, carry it over obstacles, and navigate it through the ocean, among other exercises. Each boat crew has a trainee who is the leader and receives extra attention from instructors, and each exercise is a competition that ends in a reward or penalty.

In the training thus far, there had been a highly-successful boat crew (II) and one that routinely finished last (VI). The latter was failing because they didn't work as a team and were led by a leader who seemed apathetic. The instructors decided to switch the leaders of the two boat crews, and Leif wondered if it would make a difference.

Shockingly, the usually terrible Boat Crew VI narrowly won the first race against Boat Crew II, and went on to win most of the races for the following hour. The team went from worst to first, just by switching leaders.

This illustrates "one of the most fundamental and important truths at the heart of Extreme Ownership: There are no bad teams, only bad leaders." Leadership is the most important element in performance.

Leaders must take total responsibility for their team and come up with solutions to problems that affect performance. The leader must also get the team to work together, hold them to a high standard, and relentlessly make improvements.

LESSONS

- "There are no bad teams, only bad leaders."

- Leaders must hold their teams to a high standard. Failing to do so makes low standards routine, and shielding poor performers only harms the team and the mission.

- Leaders must get a team to work together and support each other while accomplishing the mission. Leadership is the linchpin that motivates people to do this.

- If a culture of Extreme Ownership is developed within a team, the team continues to get better and can continue to perform even if the leader is absent for a time. Teams often lose leaders in combat when they are killed or wounded, but civilian organizations also lose leaders for a variety of reasons. Subordinates need to be ready to fill the gap.

- Leaders cannot become complacent. They must relentlessly try to improve themselves and their teams, and must always honestly analyze the performance of both. By spotting flaws, they continuously work to overcome them.

IN BUSINESS

Leif was contracted to coach leaders of a financial services company that had recently rolled out an unsuccessful product. The organization needed to improve, or it might fold. During the seminar, the chief technology officer (CTO) was defensive. He had been a key player in the new product and its failure was a blow to his ego. He made excuses that included blaming market factors as well as other personnel. He did not take ownership of it.

Leif related the boat crew example from BUD/S training during the seminar. He explained that because the poor leader who was originally with Boat Crew VI didn't think they could win, everyone began to think that way. He had made excuses and blamed the failure on everything else but himself. When the leaders were switched, the new leader of Boat Crew VI took Extreme Ownership. And by accepting responsibility and analyzing the team's failures, he formulated a plan to improve.

At the same time, Boat Crew II continued to perform well under the poor leader because they had residual benefits from their previous leader and success. High performance becomes the norm.

The CTO of the financial services company refused to take Extreme Ownership, however. Leif describes this type of personality as a "Tortured Genius;" someone who "accepts zero responsibility for mistakes, makes excuses, and blames everyone else for their failings (and those of their team)."

In the end, the leadership seminar went well with most of the company's leaders but not the CTO, who was initially considered too valuable—because of experience and expertise—to fire. Nevertheless, the CTO continued to complain after the seminar and resisted taking responsibility. Eventually, the company's CEO fired the CTO and a new one came on board who practiced "Extreme Ownership." The company rebounded.

This illustrates the importance of leadership, and how it is the key element of team success.

> "Often, when smaller teams within the team get so focused on their immediate tasks, they forget about what others are doing or how they depend on other teams. They may start to compete with one another, and when there are obstacles, animosity and blame develops. This creates friction that inhibits the overall team's performance. It falls on leaders to continually keep perspective on the strategic mission and remind the team that they are part of the greater team and the strategic mission is paramount."
>
> —**JOCKO WILLINK,** *Extreme Ownership: How U.S. Navy SEALs Lead and Win*

CHAPTER 3

BELIEVE

By Jocko Willink

ON HIS SECOND DEPLOYMENT to Iraq, Jocko was assigned to primarily work with Iraqi forces instead of just with SEALs and other US forces. SEALs maintain a high standard and work exceptionally well together, but his team now had to partner with troops from a less equipped military. While there were some standouts, the Iraqi soldiers often lacked food, motivation, equipment, and training.

The SEALs were tasked with training and equipping these Iraqis to fight the insurgents while fighting alongside them. Neither Jocko nor his team were happy about the mission.

Nevertheless, as a leader, he needed to project confidence and look at why the US military wanted the SEALs to do it. After analyzing the orders, Jocko realized that what amounted to "winning" in Iraq was leaving behind a stable country—and the Iraqi army needed to be good enough for this to happen.

They certainly weren't at that point, but the SEALs needed to help get them ready.

Jocko answered the "why" of the mission to believe in it himself and then communicated that rationale to convince subordinates. People who don't believe in missions lack the commitment to execute them properly and ultimately end up failing.

His team did every mission with Iraqi soldiers on that tour; and there were dangerous incidents in which SEALs were almost killed or wounded by friendly fire from Iraqi soldiers. The task was frustrating, but the Iraqis also provided some unique local knowledge which benefitted the SEALs by teaching them to better identify insurgents and navigate the area.

The Americans began to work better with the Iraqis. The SEALs and their Iraqi partners pushed insurgents out of areas and were followed by conventional US and Iraqi troops. Eventually, the Iraqi units took over many of these areas by themselves. The mission was a success.

LESSONS

- First and foremost a leader must understand the mission or objective. In order to truly understand the objective, a leader must look beyond the immediate task assigned and understand higher, strategic goals.

- Once the mission and strategy are better understood, then the leader can get behind a mission—believe in the mission. Leadership means the ability to motivate a team or unit to accomplish objectives. Belief in the mission enables a leader not only to inspire and motivate a team or unit, it also allows for smart risk-taking by a leader and the requisite buy-in from those taking the risks.

- Once this clarity is achieved, leaders must communicate this rationale to subordinates and answer their questions. Lower-level team members and junior leaders often have even less strategic perspective, and they need some of this understanding to "get" the mission. This puts goals in alignment, whether they are in combat or business.

- Don't simply explain what to do, but why the team is doing it. This motivates people.

IN BUSINESS

Jocko ran a leadership development program for a company's midlevel managers. Many of these individuals were resisting a new compensation plan that would result in lower pay. The main complaint was that the new pay structure would cause people to leave the company.

He pushed them to answer why senior leadership was putting the plan in place. No one had an answer—the midlevel managers were too intimidated to ask their senior leaders! Jocko pointed out that they would need these answers in order to be able to explain it to *their* junior leaders and other staff members.

He brought up this lack of communication with the CEO, who assumed that she would have heard about any issues. The CEO wasn't aware that subordinates would be uncomfortable with broaching difficult topics. Jocko cited the compensation plan; he told her that midlevel managers simply didn't understand the strategic purpose of the plan and thought it would cause turnover, and thus they didn't believe in it.

The CEO explained that lowering overhead would drive more sales and allow the best salespeople to potentially make more money while weeding out under-performers. After she described the strategy, he told her that she needed to do the same for her subordinates. The following day, she delivered a presentation on the new plan along with a question-and-answer session. The CEO obtained buy-in for the plan.

Afterward, Jocko taught the midlevel managers that the responsibility for asking these questions was theirs. Yes, it had been the responsibility of the CEO to explain the "why"—but it was also necessary for junior leaders to figure it out when she failed to do so. This takes courage and it is an essential part of being a leader.

A lack of buy-in from subordinates leads to failure. Extreme Ownership means that leaders at all levels are responsible for understanding the mission and higher strategy, *believing* in it, and communicating it.

> "Once people stop making excuses, stop blaming others, and take ownership of everything in their lives, they are compelled to take action to solve their problems. They are better leaders, better followers, more dependable and actively contributing team members, and more skilled in aggressively driving toward mission accomplishment. But they're also humble—able to keep their egos from damaging relationships and adversely impacting the mission and the team."
>
> **—JOCKO WILLINK,** *Extreme Ownership: How U.S. Navy SEALs Lead and Win*

CHAPTER 4

CHECK THE EGO

By Jocko Willink

JOCKO DESCRIBES AN INTENSE firefight after his base in Ramadi was attacked. The SEALs' response—rifles, grenade launchers, and belt-fed machine guns—was massive and the insurgents were repulsed. He describes the fight as a "wake-up call" to the fact that the deployment would be very dangerous.

He explains that Ramadi was the most dangerous city in Anbar, which was the most dangerous province in Iraq during 2005-2006. The ruined city was ground zero for the Sunni insurgency and thousands of insurgents controlled roughly two-thirds of it. U.S. forces conducted patrols but many outposts within Ramadi were routinely attacked by well-coordinated insurgent forces. The attacks followed a pattern: small arms fire, rocket-propelled grenades, and then mortars, followed by a suicide bomber driving a vehicle containing explosives.

Nevertheless, the author credits brave Marines and soldiers with fighting off every car-bomb attack and preventing them from getting into the outposts. Overall, his team developed immense respect for the conventional American forces they worked with.

There were some special operations units, including some SEALs, that thought of themselves as better than regular Marines and soldiers, and as a result, some conventional commanders held some animosity toward special operations units."

This friction was a problem and threatened the success of the mission. In order to overcome this problem and create a culture of cohesiveness and cooperation, Jocko's unit insisted that all team members treat conventional personnel with respect and humility.

The SEALS effectively utilized sniper fire to channel the enemy to specific locations where they would then carry out an attack. The methods they utilized were so successful that their kill count soon became noticed by higher command. Other units wanted to take part in the mission, including a similar American unit that was partnered with an elite Iraqi Army unit that operated all over the country.

This new unit wound up at a base that was run by the 101st Airborne, a conventional unit. It was a dangerous place and the commander of the 101st enforced disciplined standards that kept troops from becoming complacent. When the SEALs had been stationed there, they adhered to the same discipline and standards set for all other units. They were collaborative and respectful of all individuals regardless of what unit they belonged to. Those small gestures had gone a long way to create a synergistic culture and forge a bond between them and the other units.

The new unit exceeded the capability of the SEALs stationed there, and the Iraqi unit they worked with was better than the regular Iraqi soldiers. The SEAL platoon commander based there was afraid his team would be replaced by this unit and speculated about letting "them figure it out on their own."

Because lessons learned in combat were life and death, Jocko told the SEAL platoon commander to check his ego and work with the new unit. The platoon commander understood that trivial notions such as unit rivalry had no place within their mission and changed his attitude toward working with the new unit.

When the new unit interacted with the SEALS and conventional soldiers, however, there was friction. Unlike the SEALs, some of the new troops maintained their special operations appearance and had an arrogant and disrespectful demeanor. The SEALs, having gained a great deal of experience and knowledge, offered the unit their advice and support—the offer was ignored. Most egregious was perhaps the unit's tendency to fail to communicate their plans and coordinate with other units. In an area of operations of such complexity, this was a huge liability.

Efforts to solve the problem failed, and the 101st Airborne commander ordered the elite unit off his base within two weeks. Despite their exceptional capability, they were out of the mission.

LESSONS

- Ego is an impediment. It gets in the way of collaboration, planning, and feedback that leads to improvement.

- That said, everyone has an ego—a healthy ego can be a motivating factor; skewed too far though, it is a detriment.

- Individuals must suppress ego and be humble to practice Extreme Ownership, especially if it gets in the way of recognizing failures and fixing flaws.

- Overconfidence also breeds complacency, which in turn causes failure.

IN BUSINESS (section by Leif Babin)

Leif's company had instituted a leadership development program for the company where Gary, an operations manager worked. One day Leif received a call for help from Gary, on which he relayed that a member of his group had taken it upon himself to replace a number of key pieces of equipment without authorization. Not only had Gary's ego taken a hit by the individual's failure to consult him, but the decision had cost the company a significant amount of money due to delays.

Leif discussed the subordinate with Gary, who told him that this individual was very experienced; he also suspected the worker looked down on him, despite his position. One of Gary's concerns was that confronting him could result in the man—who was a key employee—deciding to quit.

After verifying that the worker did not intentionally cause harm to the company, Leif explained that oftentimes junior level leaders who make tactical decisions are not aware of the repercussions of their actions—they don't look at the bigger picture. Without the visibility into the overall strategy of a company, it is hard for someone to understand how certain choices can negatively affect the overall strategy. Leif advised him to address the issue and explain the situation with the full, broad viewpoint.

To communicate effectively, Leif advised the manager to own the negative impact on the company. He advised Gary to take responsibility for not communicating how decisions like those can cause costly delays. He should then discuss ways to prevent it from happening in the future. By suppressing his ego and taking the blame, he would set a good example of leadership, gain his people's—especially the specific individual's—respect, and they could move forward and formulate a solution.

Leaders are responsible for communicating the vision and overall strategy of the company to their people. And taking Extreme Ownership means not letting ego get in the way of accomplishing the mission.

PART II

THE LAWS OF COMBAT

"On any team, in any organization, all responsibility for success and failure rests with the leader. The leader must own everything in his or her world. There is no one else to blame. The leader must acknowledge mistakes and admit failures, take ownership of them, and develop a plan to win."

—**JOCKO WILLINK,** *Extreme Ownership: How U.S. Navy SEALs Lead and Win*

CHAPTER 5

COVER AND MOVE

By Leif Babin

DURING HIS TIME IN Ramadi, Leif and his unit used "overwatch" tactics—a method by which the SEALs would set up their positions up high in order to provide cover and security for units down on the ground patrolling the streets.

On this particular operation, two overwatch positions were set up, one was led by Leif. His team set off for their position at 2 a.m. but once they arrived, they found that it didn't offer a great view of the mission and the security of the building wasn't ideal. Leif explored moving the security perimeter to a second building but decided against it. He picked the best of two bad options and kept everyone in the original location.

The rest of the operation began as U.S. and Iraqi soldiers, other SEALs, and tanks moved into the neighborhood. Leif's team soon heard the other SEAL sniper team shooting at targets and they shortly joined in, firing at a group of three insurgents and hitting two. This gave away their position, so they were attacked within an hour and several times afterward. In the meantime, the operation on the ground was completed successfully and the conventional soldiers returned to base.

Usually, the SEAL overwatch teams would move back to base after sunset, but the building Leif's team was in was vulnerable. They had to decide whether to wait until nightfall to return to base, knowing the risk of being attacked while they waited was high; call armored vehicles to extract them (which could take a long time and expose the vehicles to roadside bombs); or move back to the base during daylight (which would draw attacks, though uncoordinated ones). Again, Leif had to choose the best of bad options, and he decided to immediately leave. The other SEAL team also decided to pull out before dark, though they had an easier route back to base.

Leif's team moved out onto the streets using "Cover and Move," a tactic in which the team alternates a group of men providing cover from possible threat locations while another group moves and vice versa. Within about 500 meters, the SEALs were attacked by machine-gun fire from the rear. Leif's team fired back and forced the enemy to retreat while executing their withdrawal. They made it to base without any casualties, excited about the successful operation.

Suddenly, Leif was confronted by his platoon chief, who was angry that Leif's team had decided to return to base without leaving the other SEAL sniper team in place to cover them. Leif realized his mistake; the Chief was absolutely correct. He had been so "focused on [his] squad's dilemma" that he hadn't considered the rest of the mission.

This error was fundamental. The SEALs had failed to work together fully and use all of the assets at their disposal. Leif realized he had been so caught up in detail that he had forgotten this essential principle and he resolved to use "Cover and Move" to his full advantage in the future.

LESSONS

- Cover and Move represents teamwork, and teamwork is essential in any setting. Individuals or small teams that act independently can endanger the mission.

- Divisions are common within teams, as is getting so focused on immediate tasks that one forgets about supporting players. It is a leader's job to keep teams focused on working together and accomplishing the overall mission.

- Every individual has a role to play in the mission and if the team fails, each individual fails, despite their personal performance. Blaming others is counterproductive and should be replaced by finding ways to support each other and find success. When the team wins, everyone wins.

- The mission is always the highest priority. Cover and Move—supporting each other—is critical to accomplishing it.

IN BUSINESS

Leif recounts a production manager who complained about a subsidiary owned by his parent company. The manager relied on the other company to transport product and there was friction between his subordinate leaders and theirs.

Part of the manager's mission was to reduce production downtime which cost the company money—and his team was not performing well. He blamed the subsidiary company for not moving the product fast enough. The manager claimed he could do nothing to support or improve them because they had different bosses.

Leif explained that they were all owned by the same parent company and thus had the same goal. They needed to work together to solve the issue. The production manager was exclusively worrying about his team and its problems, rather than thinking strategically as a broader team. Jocko encouraged him to communicate with the subsidiary company and create a working relationship.

The manager took the advice and found that the subsidiary had its own challenges, including a lack of resources and personnel. His team started to view the other company as partners, they worked together to solve the issues, and "the production team's downtime radically improved to industry-leading levels."

CHAPTER 6

SIMPLE

By Jocko Willink

JOCKO DESCRIBES A MORTAR attack at a combat outpost in Ramadi that killed one soldier and wounded others.

Leif and his platoon of SEALS, along with Marines and U.S. and Iraqi soldiers, had been inserted into the city to carry out a part of a larger mission with the long-term goal of clearing a highly-contested area under insurgent control. Jocko entered the city the next day with the larger force, and he was charged with the coordination between SEAL teams and other forces.

Leif and the majority of the SEALs moved out and took up a position in another building a few hundred yards away, while Army engineers fortified the new outpost. The first serious insurgent counterattack was a mortar attack, soon followed by the sound of the SEAL sniper team shooting at insurgents who were setting up to attack the outpost. The overall goal of the mission was to show local civilians and the insurgents that US and Iraqi forces were committed to securing Ramadi.

As part of this effort, a US Army advisor planned to take his unit of Iraqi soldiers out on a "presence patrol." After discussing his plan with Jocko, it became clear that the Soldier did not quite grasp how dangerous and complex the city was. In order to avoid catastrophe, Jocko convinced the Army advisor to simplify his plan, which initially included going via a long route that would take his team through very dangerous territory with a poor ability to communicate or receive back-up should it be needed.

The SEALs and soldiers prepared to move out, carefully reviewing the plans. A SEAL sniper team set up to cover their movement. Leif knew that the patrol would be attacked by insurgents and started a timer. Within 12 minutes, they were in a serious gunfight.

Two "friendlies" were wounded and needed evacuation; the patrol also required fire support. Jocko coordinated with the SEAL leader on the patrol as well as with the Army forces who would be providing help. Meanwhile, the SEAL snipers and machine gunners in the overwatch position engaged the enemy and protected the patrol. Tanks and an armored personnel carrier arrived at the patrol's position and evacuated the men; one wounded Iraqi soldier survived, while the other died.

The army advisor was rattled by his first patrol—and his first serious combat—but had fortunately agreed to the much simpler plan suggested by the SEALs.

LESSONS

- Combat (and life) is complex, and success depends on simplifying plans. Simplicity enables clarity.

- Plans must be clearly communicated in a short, direct, simple manner. Each member of the team must know their role and what to do in various scenarios. A leader who fails to communicate properly has failed to lead.

- It is also the responsibility of subordinate leaders to ask questions if they do not understand and keep asking until they do. All leaders must create an environment where this is acceptable.

- Plans and communication should be as simple as possible. Success depends on it.

IN BUSINESS

Jocko relates the story of a group of assembly technicians at a manufacturing plant who didn't understand their pay bonuses—specifically, what criteria set the amount every month. He met with the plant manager and the chief engineer the next day. Both said the plant was not as efficient as it could be, and they were surprised the bonuses didn't cause improvement. Jocko asked them to explain the bonus plan to him.

They described a very complicated system that was based on the complexity of assembling six different units. It involved applying base weights of complexity that varied when certain manufacturing targets needed to be met, as well as a "tiered efficiency metric," an assessment of the end quality of the product, and other convoluted measurements.

Jocko explained that their bonus structure was ridiculously complex and needed to be simple enough for employees to easily understand and work to achieve it. The plant manager and the chief engineer resisted the advice, as they were invested in the plan and thought the complexity was necessary.

Jocko persisted in explaining that the workers needed to have a clear connection between what they needed to strive for and the reward for doing so. The managers admitted that they hadn't seen any improvement from the bonus program—and Jocko outlined the principle of simplicity when formulating plans, emphasizing that complexity causes confusion and results in even bigger problems when things go wrong. Plans need to be simple enough to understand, which allows people to know how and what to adjust when issues come up. He provided examples from his time with the SEALs, which included everything from how they communicated to how they organized equipment.

The managers vastly simplified the bonus to measure two immediate factors (a weight of complexity and the number of units produced) along with a monthly quality assessment. The employees responded positively, productivity increased, and high performers were rewarded while low performers weeded themselves out. Overall, the efficiency gained allowed the company to do more with less—all because of a simple plan.

"As SEALs, we operate as a team of high-caliber, multitalented individuals who have been through perhaps the toughest military training and most rigorous screening process anywhere. But in the SEAL program, it is all about the Team. The sum is far greater than the parts."

—**JOCKO WILLINK,** *Extreme Ownership: How U.S. Navy SEALs Lead and Win*

CHAPTER 7

PRIORITIZE AND EXECUTE

By Leif Babin

LEIF RECOUNTS BEING IN a building in Ramadi that was being pounded by machine-gun fire and rocket-propelled grenades. After the attack died down, SEAL snipers responded and killed at least 10 insurgents. Leif moved through the building to get the status of his men.

The unit had taken the position after patrolling in through an enemy-held portion of the city. The aim was to alter insurgent operations and take the pressure off of Marine and Army outposts. Because there were so many roadside bombs, however, the SEALs knew that calling for help if they got into trouble would put rescuers at risk. Thus, they would only do so if there was no other option.

The building had good security and visibility over the area, but the team could not see the single exit and entrance well, raising the possibility that insurgents could plant explosives there without the SEALs knowing it.

The insurgents attacked the position several times during the day and the SEALs responded in turn. The combat died down at dusk and the US and Iraqi forces prepared to leave. The team's explosive ordinance disposal (EOD) personnel looked for explosives by the exit and saw a suspicious object that was later confirmed to be a bomb, which the EOD team detonated. Leif looked for a different way out of the building. The team decided to use a sledgehammer to break a hole in a concrete wall, from which the SEALs could access the rooftop of an adjacent building.

As the men were exiting through the hole in the wall onto the nearby roof, one of the SEALs fell through what had looked like a solid roof but was really a plastic tarp covering a hole—a 20' drop. The SEALS were exposed on an open roof and the stairs down to the first level were locked. They had to get down to the injured SEAL quickly. Leif started to feel overwhelmed by the pressure and the complexity of the situation facing him. He gained control of himself and allowed his training to kick in and implemented the maxim "Prioritize and Execute."

His task was to remain calm, quickly assess the situation, identify the number-one-priority, and order the team to focus on that action, followed by the next one and the next. The team executed this sequence and made it back to base. The SEAL who had fallen through the roof was mildly injured but would be ok.

LESSONS

- In battle, problems accrue and create very complex scenarios, and each issue may need a decision. Leaders must "Prioritize and Execute."

- Trying to do too many things at once leads to failure. Determining the highest priority and getting it done avoids this confusing spiral.

- Complicated, high-pressure scenarios are also common outside of combat and require a similar approach.

- One tactic to avoid this high-pressure confusion is contingency planning; mapping out reactions to potential, common issues before they happen. Leaders must game these scenarios and communicate the preferred reaction ahead of time, which enables rapid response.

- Leaders must be able to step back and remove themselves from the situation and look at it through a strategic lens. This mental distance enables effective prioritization. Leaders should also help team members set their priorities.

- Priorities may need to change quickly, depending on the situation. When this is the case, rapid and effective adaptation and communication are key.

- Leif lays out a series of steps to Prioritize and Execute:

  - Analyze the situation and identify the biggest priority.

  - Simply and clearly communicate what needs to be addressed.

  - Devise a solution and seek input from the team, if and when it's feasible.

  - Issue orders for the team to tackle and focus resources on the problem.

  - Identify the next highest priority and repeat the previous steps.

  - If priorities change, adapt and communicate the new ones quickly.

  - Keep a perspective that avoids tunnel vision. Quickly recognize and adapt to new problems.

IN BUSINESS (by Jocko Willink)

Jocko was consulting for a pharmaceutical company that was losing money. The CEO and some executives presented a briefing they had put together. The presentation was complex, containing a list of tasks that included new products, expansion into new markets, a new website, a management training program, and a revision of the sales and compensation plan to boost efficiency.

Jocko explained the concept of "decisive engagement," a military term for a force engaged in a battle that it must fight and win. The plan proposed by the company's leadership seemed like fighting multiple battles at once. Jocko pressed the CEO to prioritize—the new sales plan was named as the main goal—and then exclusively focus on that for a period to communicate the urgency to staff and make it successful.

Just as on a battlefield, when commanders get pulled in different directions and try to do too much at once, Jocko advised reorienting toward a priority, then tackling the next element of the plan, followed by the others.

The CEO agreed and spent several months prioritizing the sales plan, and this focus paid off. Prioritizing and executing put the effort on the path to success.

> *"The only meaningful measure for a leader is whether the team succeeds or fails. For all the definitions, descriptions, and characterizations of leaders, there are only two that matter: effective and ineffective. Effective leaders lead successful teams that accomplish their mission and win. Ineffective leaders do not."*
>
> **—JOCKO WILLINK,** *Extreme Ownership: How U.S. Navy SEALs Lead and Win*

CHAPTER 8

DECENTRALIZED COMMAND

By Jocko Willink

JOCKO EXPLAINS THAT COMMANDING two elements of more than 30 SEALs and the Iraqi soldiers they worked with in a complex battlespace would have been impossible without using the concept of Decentralized Command. Subordinate leaders must be able to take initiative and make sound decisions, and as a higher-level leader, Jocko needed to defer to and trust their judgment. He and other leaders had trained the SEALs to take this initiative and they did, enabling Jocko to pay attention to strategy.

Utilizing a Decentralized Command methodology requires a knowledge of and confidence in junior leaders' capabilities, a great deal of trust, and an ability to surrender control. For it to work, leaders at all levels need to have a good grasp of the vision, fully understand the mission, its objective, and how to fulfill it.

To prepare for Iraq, the SEALs underwent training in a mock-up of a city. It involved putting the trainees through a variety of confusing and surprising scenarios. Initially, some of the leaders attempted to control all aspects of the mission. This is impossible to do successfully in a complex combat environment, and they soon learned to put faith in their subordinate leaders. The first critical step was to ensure that each of his junior leaders fully understood the mission and the overall Commander's Intent. Then each individual leader could focus on his direct reports and their part of the overall plan, each direct report could then only focus on their direct reports and their individual jobs, etc. SEALs were expected to formulate plans and execute them on their own within this sphere of control.

This structure worked well on the deployment to Ramadi. Jocko describes a large, complex operation involving two Army battalions, one Marine battalion, the SEALs, almost 100 vehicles, and air assets, some using their own communications networks. The SEALs were tasked with entering the area first and establishing overwatch positions. Jocko was in charge of the coordination between all forces. The operation took place in a particularly violent part of the city where one SEAL had previously been killed and several wounded.

The SEAL teams entered the city at night, communicating their positions to Jocko, who had allowed them to determine where they would set up for the operation and adapt those plans if necessary.

The maps were not always accurate and sometimes initial locations needed to be changed on the fly. In these cases, the leaders on the ground just adapted and communicated the revision to Jocko. One of the SEAL platoons had to change their originally planned position and selected a new building on this mission. Reports of enemy forces preparing to attack poured in, including a report from a unit of Army armored vehicles that a team of enemy snipers was on the roof of a building.

Jocko verified that the building the soldiers targeted was not the one where the SEALs were positioned. But he asked for additional verification before the armored vehicles opened fire. His caution was rewarded: the original building had been misidentified and US troops had almost fired on the SEALs.

Decentralized Command had played a role in preventing this tragedy. Because Jocko trusted his leaders in the field to manage the tactical details, it freed him up to focus on his job: putting all of his attention on coordinating the friendly forces. Without this focus, he might have missed this last-second call.

LESSONS

- Humans can only manage so much complexity. Teams should be no more than four or five people immediately managed by a leader.

- Within this structure, subordinate leaders must understand the mission and the Commander's Intent and have the latitude to make decisions that fulfill it.

Leaders must also understand the "why"—not just the "how."

- Teams must be organized according to tasks and led by leaders with clear goals.

- Leaders must intuitively understand exactly what is within their authority when making decisions.

- Subordinate leaders must constantly communicate decisions to upper leaders, as well as recommended courses of action for decisions that are outside of their responsibility. In turn, higher leaders must actively communicate down the chain of command.

- Junior leaders must take initiative and be proactive, and leaders at all levels must trust each other.

- Leaders must strike an appropriate balance between trying to control too much and becoming too disconnected from what is happening on the front lines.

IN BUSINESS

Jocko asked a regional president of an investment advisor group to show him an organizational chart of his team. Jocko reviewed it and saw that it was disorganized. In particular, one manager of a branch led 21 people, and another led two.

The president explained that branches grew based on the effectiveness of their managers, but that their efficiency slowed after reaching a certain size, at which point he noted a lack of focus on the overall strategy. Smaller branches conversely didn't grow in the first place because the managers had to focus on generating revenue rather than strategy. The president estimated that five or six people would be ideal for a team, which mirrors the organizational structure of teams in the military.

Jocko explained how decentralized command can be an effective way of leading teams of more than 100 individuals. You would need to assign a manager a team of five or six junior leaders, each of whom would be responsible for a team of five or six individuals and so forth. This mode of organization requires that each subordinate leader communicate very clear commands and guidance down the chain and executing the mission with appropriate discretion. Jocko also explained the importance of a clearly-understood mission and setting boundaries for behavior to keep the organization in sync.

Also essential is the element of trust, which enables leaders to cede control and avoid micromanaging. Trust also lets subordinates know that they have the latitude to act and they will receive support from leaders when necessary. It takes time and experience, including the freedom to fail a little, for this trust to build. The president agreed to implement a decentralized command structure.

> *"The goal of all leaders should be to work themselves out of a job. This means leaders must be heavily engaged in training and mentoring their junior leaders to prepare them to step up and assume greater responsibilities. When mentored and coached properly, the junior leader can eventually replace the senior leader, allowing the senior leader to move on to the next level of leadership."*
>
> —**JOCKO WILLINK,** *Extreme Ownership: How U.S. Navy SEALs Lead and Win*

PART III

SUSTAINING VICTORY

> "If the plan is simple enough, everyone understands it, which means each person can rapidly adjust and modify what he or she is doing. If the plan is too complex, the team can't make rapid adjustments to it, because there is no baseline understanding of it."
>
> —**JOCKO WILLINK,** *Extreme Ownership: How U.S. Navy SEALs Lead and Win*

CHAPTER 9

PLAN

By Leif Babin

LEIF WRITES OF A hostage rescue mission in Ramadi. SEALs were tasked with rescuing the kidnapped teenage nephew of an Iraqi police colonel. The SEALs had information on where he was being held; it was in a difficult area that was controlled by insurgents and mined with improvised explosive devices (IEDs).

The SEALs planned the mission: a team of snipers would move in first to watch the target and cover an assault team that would rush the house, clear it, and rescue the hostage. After running the plan by the commander of Army forces and briefing the men who would execute it, the SEALs suddenly received new intelligence: the yard of the target house was filled with bombs and a bunker with a machine gun was inside. Despite this new danger, the SEALs moved ahead with the plan, which relied on speed and surprise.

It was a success. The SEALs quickly took over and cleared the house, capturing the insurgents and rescuing the hostage without firing any shots.

Later, while working as a SEAL leadership instructor, Leif utilized this mission as a teaching exercise. He ran through the planning steps and then informed the class about the sudden intelligence about new threats. He asked the students what they would do, and responses included aborting the mission or changing the plan.

Leif pointed out that those threats could be present on any mission, and a good leader had to always plan for such contingencies. Mission planning must never take things for granted and always work to minimize risk by using a standardized planning process.

LESSONS

- Analyzing and understanding the mission is the first step in planning. This must result in clear, simple directives and goals.

- Those executing a mission must explicitly understand its purpose. This Commander's Intent is the framework for decisions made at all levels.

- Planners must consider various options to accomplish the mission with available resources. Sufficient information must then be gathered while relying on subject matter experts and others with relevant experience.

- Leaders should delegate much of the planning to subordinate leaders, and personnel at all levels should have a say and ownership of their particular aspect of a plan. This promotes investment in the plan, which leads to more successful execution.

- Leaders cannot get lost in the details of a plan and must focus on the bigger elements.

- When a plan is created, it must be communicated clearly and directly, and both this briefing and the planning itself should be a give and take in which all team members can ask questions and discuss it.

- All team members must understand:

    - The strategic mission

    - The Commander's Intent

    - The team's mission

    - Each team member's role

    - Contingencies

- Leaders must be comfortable with some amount of risk but work to reduce it through contingency planning.

- Teams must analyze what worked and didn't about any plan after it is executed to improve future plans.

- The planning process should be standardized so that support teams can understand it and it is a repeatable process. This involves using common terminology and a checklist of general steps that should be accounted for.

IN BUSINESS

A vice president of emerging markets for a company had seen great success when putting experienced individuals into new areas and letting them devise plans, and he now wanted to standardize this process. One of his subordinates, a regional manager, didn't seem to buy into the effort needed to develop a process. Leif explained how he learned to rely on and properly execute planning as a SEAL.

Military mission briefs, also known as operations orders (OPORD) enumerate the steps in a mission. These are vital, as they clearly inform the people who execute and support what will be required in order to accomplish it. In Leif's SEAL training, there were routine problems with the plans and briefings formulated by trainees. Notably, building long PowerPoint presentations wasted time that could have been spent creating a better plan.

While training for deployment to Ramadi, Leif and the other SEALs had to learn how to use the standard OPORD planning process effectively. Two of the three SEAL task units would be deployed to combat and a third to a mostly non-combat deployment in the Philippines. All wanted to deploy to Iraq, and they would be judged by their performance, especially on the briefing for the last field exercise.

Leif's team worked hard on the brief, but it was too long and Power Point-heavy. Jocko advised them to focus on making the plan clear and simple for the SEALs who would execute it rather than trying to impress the upper leaders who would evaluate it. They vastly simplified it and focused on communicating the Commander's Intent so the rest of the team could fill in the details. This enabled the leaders to focus on the big picture and catch mistakes, and subordinates to take ownership of their part of the plan.

Leif's task unit conducted a successful briefing and it was chosen to deploy to Iraq, where they further developed and refined a standardized planning process that was crucial to operating successfully in a very complex and difficult combat environment.

Leif emphasized to the company what a valuable resource it would be for them to implement a standardized process that could be used by all departments in their organization. He provided them a template based on the military OPORD process and they tailored it to their business. Key leaders in the emerging markets team then used this framework to devise a plan in a common business scenario, followed by a briefing to leaders, critique session, and revision.

The regional manager—who had been skeptical of standardizing plans—now saw the value in it. She explained that when they had executed the plan, it had allowed them to have contingencies in place that saved revenue, and Commander's Intent enabled decisiveness among subordinates.

CHAPTER 10

LEADING UP AND DOWN THE CHAIN OF COMMAND

By Leif Babin

LEIF MENTIONS REFLECTING ON the SEALs deployment to Ramadi, Iraq. While the tour had been action-packed and successful, they had lost two SEALs, and another had been shot in the face and lost his eyesight. Nevertheless, the SEALs and their US Army partners had made a difference, improving security and setting the area on a path to continued progress.

Leif felt immense responsibility for not bringing all of his men home and became angry at a media that didn't understand the real sacrifices—as well as those in the SEAL community who criticized his team's efforts. These critics didn't understand the nature of the counterinsurgency fight and how it differed from traditional special operations, nor what an impact this unique strategy had made in Ramadi.

Jocko was tasked with creating a presentation for the most senior admiral in the Navy that showed what they had accomplished. It included a map that illustrated how many enemy-held neighborhoods in Ramadi the SEALs had recouped. The slide was powerful and impressed upon Leif that he had been so focused on immediate details that he hadn't fully understood the magnitude of the results. He also realized that his men didn't understand it either—he had failed to explain this impact to them.

Leif noted that the SEALs who tended to grow tired of the mission and question it were those who had the least involvement—ownership—in the planning aspect, whereas those who were involved during the planning phase tended to stay more engaged and had a better understanding of the overall picture. He determined that he could have done more to "lead down the chain of command:" providing more subordinates ownership of actions, asking more questions to get clarity, and communicating what he learned as well as the impact of the strategy.

LESSONS

- Leaders are responsible for leading a team toward a strategic goal. While subordinates do not need to focus on the big picture and leaders do not need to know all of the details, each must understand what the other is doing.

- Leaders must communicate overall strategy regularly, so subordinates can understand their role and how to prioritize.

- Leaders sometimes don't appreciate that subordinates don't have this perspective or understanding of the strategy.

- This communication should involve direct contact, conversations, and observation of subordinates to understand their point of view and clarify the Commander's Intent if needed.

- If a team is not performing as expected, a leader must take ownership and judge whether the problem is due to a lack of adequate communication.

In Ramadi, Leif had become angry at an email from higher headquarters that asked for obvious details about a mission plan they were about to execute.

Jocko had previously complained about questions like this but had eventually realized that superiors were simply after information they didn't have.

He explained to Leif that providing this information gave higher leaders what they needed to comfortably approve operations. Jocko also realized that leading up the chain of command meant providing enough information to leaders so they wouldn't have to ask questions with *seemingly* obvious answers. Both men took ownership and realized that they needed to communicate better to give their leaders the information they needed.

They began writing more detailed plans and reports and invited leaders to their area to accompany them on missions. The commanding officer and his staff began to understand what the SEALs in Ramadi were doing and a trust started to build—subsequently every mission was approved.

LESSONS

- Rather than instinctively becoming frustrated with senior leaders' inability to make decisions in a timely manner, first assess whether this delay is being caused by a lack of detail in information that you should be providing. If this is the case, adapt your communication pattern.

- Effectively communicating the situation—detailed, fact-based explanations of problems and your needs—will go a long way to influence senior leadership and will often yield the desired results.

- Leaders must be cognizant of the fact that senior leaders also have to deal with limitations, shifts in direction, and unforeseen issues on their end.

- Leaders must **always** support *their* leaders. Voicing dissent or discord about senior leaders, or their decisions and directives in front of subordinates is counterproductive at best and hugely pernicious at worst.

- If you do not understand a directive, ask questions until you do. Once the debate about a decision is over and an order is given, carry it out with enthusiasm.

IN BUSINESS

A field manager of a company explained how leadership at corporate HQ—located hundreds of miles away—didn't understand the issues in the field. He believed that the routine questions and paperwork distracted his team from executing plans. Leif explained how he'd dealt with similar oversight in Iraq, including having to submit all plans for approval and detailed debriefings after missions.

Leif provided two options: giving up and complaining or finding a way to move forward within this framework.

He asked the manager if leadership wanted him to fail and the man answered "no," which meant they simply wanted information. Under the concept of Extreme Ownership, a leader must realize that it is his or her responsibility to communicate. Leif advised the manager to ask questions about the purpose of requests and plans, and to communicate when something caused hardship or didn't work well ***and offer a***

solution. In addition, the manager should invite senior leaders to see the operation in person.

The manager adapted, sending extremely detailed information to leadership and hosting them on a trip to observe and meet his team. This visit forged a better relationship and helped communicate challenges while giving the manager greater respect for his bosses.

CHAPTER 11

DECISIVENESS AMID UNCERTAINTY

By Leif Babin

LEIF DESCRIBES AN INCIDENT in Ramadi involving fellow SEAL Chris Kyle, one of the most effective snipers in US military history. Kyle radioed Leif that he had a potential target, having seen someone with a weapon in the window of a building. This communication was unusual since Kyle had the authority to shoot any enemy fighter that he could positively identify with a weapon and hostile intent. The fact that he called Leif over meant he was unsure.

The SEAL team had once again entered into the city ahead of a large conventional force to provide cover as they cleared buildings. It was therefore important that Leif make sure that the individual Kyle had spotted wasn't a US soldier. Adding to the pressure was the fact that enemy snipers had been killing and wounding US troops, so there was a huge emphasis on stopping them.

Leif called the commander of the US Army forces that were conducting the clearing mission to verify that none of his troops were in that specific building. In order to clearly identify buildings and positions, they were each given a specific numerical code. The company commander said there were none and requested that the SEALs shoot the potential sniper. Leif and Kyle waited, still unable to identify the man as an enemy threat. The US Army commander again asked the SEALs to shoot.

Leif weighed how important it was to eliminate enemy snipers and the guilt he would feel if he'd failed to do so and the insurgent later killed US troops versus the consequences of killing a US soldier and decided he couldn't live with himself if he ordered the shot.

He declined the company commander's request and asked that he send troops to clear the building with the suspected sniper. After a back and forth, the exasperated company commander ordered his troops to send men to re-clear the building. When they moved out to do it, Leif realized the error: they had misidentified the building.

The man in the window had in fact been a US soldier. Kyle had been spared the repercussions of having been ordered to take the shot.

LESSONS

- Combat leaders deal with immense pressure stemming from "uncertainty, chaos, and the element of the unknown." These individuals must often act without complete information in an environment where decisions have huge consequences. They must act decisively and never be frozen by fear.

- There is seldom a completely flawless decision. Leaders must accept this reality and still make decisions quickly.

- Gathering information is a crucial part of any plan, however, leaders must recognize that there will never be enough data to guarantee success, yet decisions still need to be made.

- Leif refers to this as the "'incomplete picture' principle" and notes that although common in personal and business situations, the consequences are not usually life and death, but they can be severe. Nevertheless, leaders must get used to uncertainty and act decisively.

IN BUSINESS

Leif and Jocko were providing leadership coaching to a successful software company and one of its subsidiaries, an engineering company. The CEO of the engineering company was under pressure from competitors looking to poach talented engineers from her successful team. The worry was that the loss of an engineer would, in turn, mean the loss of that engineer's team.

Complicating the situation was the rivalry between two engineers vying for promotion that had become very intense. They argued, criticized each other, and worked against each other. The CEO of the engineering company had tried to defuse the conflict to no avail and the situation was harming the overall team.

The conflict came to a head when both engineers insisted the other be fired and claimed that their competitor was planning to leave the company.

Jocko asked the CEO which of the claims by the two engineers she believed; she wasn't sure. Though she was disturbed by the possibility of the engineers leaving and taking members of their team with them, she decided to wait and see what happened. This went against the SEALs' instincts, as they were trained to act decisively. Jocko and Leif gamed scenarios with the CEO, including asking what she thought might happen and the possibility of firing one of them. Jocko then suggested another option: firing both of them.

Shocked, the engineering CEO protested that she didn't even want to lose one and the loss of two would be terrible. Jocko pointed out that neither man was a good leader and the CEO hadn't thought many members of their teams were particularly loyal to them. Some of these individuals could take their places.

Also, the leadership needed to be seen as decisive and not being willing to be held hostage to demands. Finally, the SEALs made the point that the terrible attitude of these individuals was contagious and could do long-term harm to the company.

The CEOs of both companies agreed. After identifying two replacements from within the teams, they fired both senior engineers.

"The Dichotomy of Leadership...

A good leader must be:
- *confident but not cocky;*
- *courageous but not foolhardy;*
- *competitive but a gracious loser;*
- *attentive to details but not obsessed by them;*
- *strong but have endurance;*
- *a leader and follower;*
- *humble not passive;*
- *aggressive not overbearing;*
- *quiet not silent;*
- *calm but not robotic, logical but not devoid of emotions;*
- *close with the troops but not so close that one becomes more important than another or more important than the good of the team; not so close that they forget who is in charge.*
- *able to execute Extreme Ownership, while exercising Decentralized Command.*

A good leader has nothing to prove, but everything to prove."

—JOCKO WILLINK, *Extreme Ownership: How U.S. Navy SEALs Lead and Win*

CHAPTER 12

DISCIPLINE EQUALS FREEDOM— THE DICHOTOMY OF LEADERSHIP

By Jocko Willink

JOCKO DESCRIBES "'CAPTURE/KILL' MISSIONS" on his first deployment to Iraq which involved assaulting a target based on intelligence and ideally capturing insurgents to obtain intelligence. One thing the SEALs weren't prepared for as warfighters: they had to gather evidence that would hold up in a local court to convict suspected terrorists.

Initially, their methods of searching a house were haphazard and destructive, resulting in some evidence being overlooked—it also took too long. The Iraqi courts also eventually imposed even more meticulous requirements for evidence collection.

Jocko ordered his assistant platoon commander to come up with a more efficient way to search targets and gather evidence. He created a plan that was complex overall but broken down into individuals doing simple tasks; hypothetically this would make the process more efficient and thoroughly document the evidence collection. When it was briefed to his SEAL team, however, there was pushback. Jocko explained why they needed to do this, pointing out the issues with current methods, and the team reluctantly agreed to test the new procedure. A test run yielded much faster searches and the team bought into it.

When it was rolled out in combat, the method vastly increased speed, enabling the SEALs to conduct multiple missions per night while improving the quality of the evidence collected. The new process was an example of "discipline equals freedom," according to Jocko.

He explains that the first test of an individual's discipline is making the decision to get out of bed very early in the morning—and small decisions like this translate into bigger impacts on your life. The best SEALs tended to get up and start work early, constantly improve their skills, and "make time" to do extra tasks that are deemed important. This constant discipline improves how they perform—which again, results in *more freedom.*

Jocko always attempted to improve his personal discipline and that of his teams. Being disciplined about using standard operating procedures (SOPs) enables Decentralized Command, allowing teams more latitude to make better decisions. Disciplined teams win; and Jocko created a culture of extreme discipline, improving and practicing many SOPs on his later deployment to Iraq—from how the SEALs communicated to how they reacted to the enemy.

It freed the SEALs up to be more adaptable and revise plans, and Jocko explains that the discipline needed to create this freedom is a balancing act; some teams take discipline so far that they lose flexibility. Successful ones strike the right balance.

LESSONS

- Leaders must strike a balance between seemingly opposite principles like discipline (standard operating procedures) and freedom (decentralized command).

- Leaders must be willing to follow more knowledgeable or better-situated subordinates at times. Confident leaders put aside ego to do this.

- Leaders must strike a balance between being aggressive and too aggressive. And subordinates must feel comfortable bringing up issues or valid disagreements.

- Leaders must show emotion but control it. Unemotional leaders can't connect with those they lead, while highly-emotional leaders lose respect.

- Leaders should be "confident but never cocky" and courageous but never foolishly so. Leaders must possess a bias for action, and therefore leaders cannot, under any circumstances, be passive.

- Jocko outlines more "Leadership Dichotomies:"
  - Have attention to details but don't get caught up in them
  - Show strength but also focus on endurance
  - Quiet leadership is valuable; silent leadership is not
  - Establish bonds with those led but maintain enough distance so there is no question who is in command
  - Practice Extreme Ownership *and* Decentralized Command

IN BUSINESS

A CFO of a construction company explained to Jocko that the organization's electrical division was losing money and likely would continue to do so for at least five years. The CFO thought the division should be closed and speculated that the reason it had not been was because the head of the division was an old friend of the CEO.

Jocko met with the CEO the following day and discussed the electrical division and the problems keeping it open could cause, as explained by the CFO. Eventually, the executive admitted that he was keeping it open because of his friendship with the head of the division.

Jocko explained how one of the dichotomies of leadership applied to the situation: a leader must get to know his people on a personal level; care for his people and their well-being, but not become overly close with any of them. Being overly involved or attached could result in a leader's inability to make tough decisions. Mission accomplishment is the number one priority for all leaders. Sometimes a leader's greatest qualities can be a weakness, and, in this case, the CEO's loyalty was clouding his judgment.

Soon after, the CEO began the shutdown of the unprofitable division; his friend took the news professionally and accepted another position in the company. This difficult decision was the right one for the company.

OTHER BOOKS BY CHRIS LAMBERTSEN

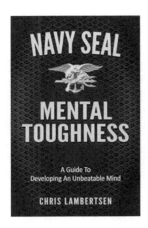

Navy SEAL Mental Toughness: A Guide To Developing An Unbeatable Mind

https://amzn.to/2xpb2JY

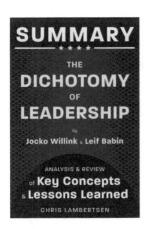

Summary of The Dichotomy of Leadership: Balancing the Challenges of Extreme Ownership by Jocko Willink and Leif Babin

amazon.com/dp/0989822974

DO YOU HAVE A MINUTE TO HELP ME OUT?

Dear Reader,

Thank you for taking the time to read this summary of *Extreme Ownership: How US Navy SEALs Lead and Win* by Jocko Willink and Leif Babin. I hope you found it useful, insightful and enjoyable.

If you have a minute, could you help me out by leaving a review on Amazon?

Your review is incredibly important to the success of this summary on Amazon. It only takes a few moments, and I would be deeply grateful for your support.

If you've never left a review before, it's super simple:

STEP 1: Type the following link in a browser:

https://amzn.to/3czUpdG

STEP 2: Sign into Amazon if you aren't already signed in.

STEP 3: Choose your star rating and write a review. It doesn't have to be long, even a few words will do. The title is optional, so feel free to leave it blank.

Thank you for your help and support! It means a lot to me!

Best regards,
Chris Lambertsen

Made in United States
Troutdale, OR
03/12/2024